The art of deep listening

Cultivating Awareness, Presence, and Connection through Listening and Rattling Practices

The art of deep listening

CULTIVATING AWARENESS,
PRESENCE, AND CONNECTION
THROUGH LISTENING AND
RATTLING PRACTICES

DANIEL TIGNER

WITH CONTRIBUTIONS FROM TOMSON HIGHWAY,
UNMANI LENGER AND SEAN WALKING BEAR

Daniel Tigner, Inquiry Books
www.inquirybooks.com
Email: info@inquirybooks.com

Title:

The Art of Deep Listening Cultivating Awareness, Presence, and Connection through Listening and Rattling Practice

Format: Hardcover book

This publication has been assigned: ISBN 978-1-9990685-8-5

Text:
Daniel Tigner

Cover and Book Design
Amanda Tupiná

Rattling Painting:
Julie Sutton

Photos:
Daniel Tigner, unless
otherwise noted

Images of rattles:
Public Domain, from the
collection of the Metropolitan
Museum of Art, New York
(https://metmuseum.org/)

ACKNOWLEDGEMENTS

Thanks to my sweetheart, Maryse Cohen, for her careful readings of the book and thoughtful feedback.

Thanks to my dear friend, Saroja Poilblan, for sharing her experience of rattling and reviewing this text.

Thank you to my friend, Unmani Lenger, who agreed to be interviewed on Shamanic and Soul Work with the rattle.

I am grateful to Sean Walking Bear, a true artisan and master rattle maker, for his agreeing to tell about his work and life experience.

A special thanks to Tomson Highway, author, playwright, composer and pianist, for sharing his profoundly lived experience of silence.

"Really listening and love are the same."

John de Ruiter

PREFACE

This book is meant to be compact and useful to those interested in sound, listening and rattling as a gateway to the soul, higher consciousness and being fully present. While writing it, the question has been, "What insights and practical directions might enable you to more fully explore sound, listening and rattling for healing, dream awareness, release, meditations and answers to questions?"

INTRODUCTION

Sound and soul interweave. Sound expresses soul.

In Part 1 of this book, we explore sound and soul and listening meditations. Sound meditations are natural and easy and with the right understanding, listening brings awareness, and presence.

Part 2 is about the many dimensions of the rattle and rattling. The rattle is one of the most ancient and intuitively used instruments: rhythms, beats and silence inducing trance states for soul journeying, and integration and harmonizing of different parts of ourselves. Rattling is a valuable tool in healing and manifestation work.

"The word 'listen' contains the same letters as the word 'silent'."

Alfred Brendel

"Listening means both you and your ears are present, connected – then listening happens. It is a difficult matter. To create the connection with the ears is a matter of spiritual endeavor. Listening means that when you are hearing, your whole consciousness becomes the hearing; only the hearing remains, nothing else."

Osho, Finger Pointing to the Moon

PART 1

LISTENING
MEDITATIONS

MEDITATIONS ON SOUND

We are surrounded by sounds emanating from close to us (i.e. in our own body) to all around us in our environment. We can follow our heartbeat or listen to the sound of our breathing or to the ticking of the clock on the wall.

There are many sound exercises and activities that open specific doors of perception, relaxation and well being from rattling to drumming, tuning in to natural sounds or listening to sacred music, reciting mantras or hearing Gregorian chants, singing and humming. Here's a list of some activities or exercises with sounds:

Opening to the vastness, yoga teacher Cathia in a perfect pose.

What to listen to

What are the
sounds of a male
Wood Duck (*Aix
sponsa*) in spring?

— Listen to the sounds of your body

— Listen to your breathing

— Listen to the sounds of sleep

— Listen to sounds of your environment

— Listen to the birds singing

— Listen to the wind

— Listen to the sound of running water

— Listen to waves in the ocean

— Listen to the sounds of the city

— Listen to the radio

— Listen to bells striking and sounds fading

— Listen to people

— Listen to animal friends

— Listen to sacred music

— Listen to a baby

— Listen to children playing

— Listen to Gregorian chants

— Listen to the gentle sounds of the falling pebbles in a Rain Stick

— Listen to the strong rhythmic sounds of the rattle

— Listen to humming – hum with lips closed

— Listen to Tibetan overtone singing – a kind of deep chant

— Listen to a mantra

— Listen to the blowing of the Shofar

— Listen to crickets singing in the evening

— Listen to the gaps between sounds

— Listen to the call to prayer (Adhan) if you live near a mosque

— Listen to the fading sound of a bell or gong

— Listen to the vibrating melding sounds of string instruments

— Listen to blasts of a trumpet

— Listen to the soothing sounds of an oboe

— Listen to OM

— Listen to meditative music, feel the core or essence of the music

— Every moment sound and silence surround you. Truly listen.

How to Listen

— Just relax, listen attentively.

— Listen in an unfocused manner, being receptive to all sounds.

— Or focus on certain sounds: a musical instrument, birds, your breath...

— Or listen to wherever your attention alights, like a bee going from flower to flower.

— Or listen to the silence between sounds. the gaps between words, the silence between notes...

— Or listen to a striking sound.

— Or listen to fading sounds into silence.

— Listen to oceanic sounds.

— Listen to rhythms and harmonies.

— Listen to sounds you create singing, humming, harmonies...

— Listen to the "green" sounds from nature such as rain falling, ocean waves, leaves rustling (green noise uses a consistent mid-level frequency to produce a steady sound).

— Explore and enjoy the many aspects of listening...

All Our Senses Are Doors

Listening is a marvellous way to return to our inner source but
know that all our 5 senses are doors. You might see a beautiful
flower, hear the whisper of the breeze and smell its aroma all
at the same time. When making popcorn, you might listen
to it popping, smell it and taste it. When you are receiving a
back rub, you might both feel and hear the movement of hands

and fingers gliding over your skin. A child smiles at you and giggles with joy, let both sight and sound touch your heart. Like a bee going from flower to flower, allow your attention to alight where it will. Let your senses be vividly alive and hold you in the moment!

Each sense can bring us in towards our being or out towards the world. When we listen with presence we move inwardly, and all the other senses become heightened. Touch is more sensitive, taste subtler and more filling, beautiful aromas delight us, and colors seem more intense, shapes and textures more defined...

Sounds of the Day

If you listen attentively to the moment to moment sounds throughout your day, you will find yourself being more silent and present, less in the mind (and its traffic, inner noise), more in the heart.

You will become more conscious of being conscious, easily recalling that there is an awareness that is aware of it all.

It will be much easy then to remember "I am."

When God spoke to Moses, he said that his name is "I am that I am." When we relax in the awareness of our own being, I am, we can feel ourselves being part of the great I am. We are aware of the divine intelligence that pervades all and which is prior to all.

"I frequently hear music in the very heart of noise."

George Gershwin

THE QUALITY OF SOUND

Music

Sometimes, listen to great music with total presence, letting it fill you. Discover the music that is sacred and nourishes your heart and being.

A woman playing the Theoro-Lute with a cavalier, oil on wood, painted by the Dutch artist Gerard ter Borch the Younger, circa 1658.
"In this intimate scene, a young woman strums a lute while playing a duet with her suitor. Songbooks, such as the one lying on the table here, were common lovers' gifts at the time. The watch lying alongside it may symbolize temperance, or perhaps the fleeting nature of the affair."
Source: Metropolitan Museum, New York
Image Public Domain

Transforming Unpleasant Sounds

What is our inner attitude when we hear certain sounds around us? Does the heavy breathing or snoring of someone at night disturb us? Do the sounds of the city grate on our nerves? Whether a sound is perceived as noise or as music has much to do with our mind frame. One key is to change the sound gestalt, our inner attitude towards sound, by welcoming all the sounds around us. Listening to any sound can bring us to the moment - just about any sound can be music.

What then, if anything, should we do with harsh, invasive sounds such as a dripping faucet, chainsaws, construction, road traffic, loud radios, the clunk-clunk of footsteps on the floor above us, screaming neighbors or the TV next door? We can try to block it (earplugs), override it with something more pleasant, neutralize it with white noise, put on our earphones and tune in to something else. Sometimes noise is just pollution, and we should move away if we can.

At times though, especially as we make listening part of our daily way of being, we can listen to so-called noise just as we listen to pleasant sounds, just like as when we listen to music or the singing of birds.

Exploring possibilities of transforming 'noise' can be an exciting and challenging inner adventure, with moments of delightful reward! Speaking of finding music in the sounds of the city, the composer George Gershwin (1898 to 1937) created wonderful music incorporating realistic sound effects from everyday life in *Rhapsody in Blue* and *An American in Paris*.

Sound and Brain States

Many musicians have created music and soundscapes to induce specific brainwave states conducive to relaxation, meditation, and focus. Other creators have incorporated such music and background sounds to induce brain waves that make us more receptive to their guided meditations and hypnosis.

Brain Wave Frequency	Frequency Range	State
Beta (β)	12–35 Hz	activities, external attention
Alpha (α)	8–12 Hz	relaxed, passive attention, creativity
Theta (θ)	4–8 Hz	deep relaxation, inwardly focused
Delta (δ)	0.5–4 Hz	deep, dreamless sleep, also during REM (Rapid Eye Movement) sleep

Remember that a certain brainwave pattern may occur in meditation, but it is not the cause of meditation, by which we mean a state of awareness in which you are conscious of being conscious, presence prior to thoughts and body-mind-emotions activities....

"When people talk, listen completely.
Most people never listen."

Ernest Hemingway

Maryse reading to Sepporah, who at the time was 5-months old. On the page in the book Maryse is holding, the text reads, "We'll sing and dance and laugh and cry."

LISTENING TO OTHERS

Listening to Your Child

Listen to your child with your presence. Listen to your child's soul. Whenever you can take your time, listen and observe. You will be fulfilling a deep need of your child, to be truly heard, felt and seen! And, because you are present to your child, your actions will be responses to your child's and your own needs.

Listen to Your Friend, Lover or Partner with Totality

This is a way of honouring your beloved, of harmonizing your energies, of understanding more about them and your Self. Listen not just to what they say, but to their being, their soul!

Put aside anything you know about your partner, put aside your thoughts, your reactive nature and simply listen with totality. See and feel them and appreciate them with fresh ears and eyes!

Listen to Your Dog, Cat or Animal Friend

What does your animal friend need? How are they feeling? How is their health? Listening can tell us many things and deepen your knowing, understanding and enjoyment of your friend.

The quality of listening must be one of the secrets of an animal whisperer.

When we listen fully and totally, feeling the consciousness and beingness of an animal, a deep empathy naturally arises.

"My music comes out of silence."

Tomson Highway in conversation

SOUNDS WHILE IN ACTIVITIES

Cathia and Eliot, yoga teachers, in prayerful stillness, in Aylmer, Quebec, Canada (centreyogaaylmer. com)

Listening to Your Breathing and Body Sounds

Body-mind-emotions are a continuum linked by and reflected in your breathing. When you are upset, your breathing is rougher and more erratic, while when you are at peace it becomes calmer, slower and more rhythmic. The awareness that arises when we listen to our breathing and body sounds teaches us about our body-mind-emotions, giving us greater input into our health as we become attuned to our own body-mind-emotional needs.

As a meditation, sit comfortably with a straight back, close your eyes and simply listen to your breathing, allowing it to become calmer, smoother, more and more silent. Try this for 20 minutes everyday for a month. Notice what happens during this time and at the end of the month how awareness of breathing has evolved. Do you feel more in tune?

When we are aware and centered simply by listening to our breathing and body sounds, we tend to be less reactive and more responsive, less stressed, less taken in by outside pressures, less identified....

And, this awareness through listening is available to us anytime, anywhere!!!

Listen During Vigorous Activity Such as a Sport

Enjoy the engine of the body at work, its power, the energy being channeled and released, the phases as you warm-up, engage, move in spurts and make great efforts. Listen and be absorbed in the whole process of life energy working in you!

Take your workout to another level!

Common loon (*Gavia immer*)
Photo : Daniel Tigner

Listen When You Are Making Love

Listening fully will bring another dimension to love making,
more presence, more sensitivity and attunement between you
and your partner. Sounds carry so much energy, listening
while making love is so sensual, such a powerful aphrodisiac!

Sleeping Boy, Terracotta painted white, Philippe Laurent Roland, France, 1774, created by artist while in Rome. Source: Metropolitan Museum, New York
Image Public Domain

Listen to the Sounds of Sleep

Listen to yourself as you fall into sleep. Listen to your bed partner throughout the night. Listen to your child sleeping. What can you learn? Are there sleep habits that you can identify? Can it help you to sleep better? Can it support entering sleep with awareness?

Certain soundscapes and music in the theta and delta range are potentially helpful in promoting a better night's sleep.

"I merely took the energy it takes to pout and wrote some blues."

Duke Ellington

LISTENING TO WISDOM

Listen to a Reading of a Spiritual Text or a Prayer

There are many beautiful readings of spiritual texts, such as from the Koran, Bible, Torah, or texts from Buddhism or Hinduism.

Listen to whatever texts you feel connected to with presence, feeling the tone, rhythm and texture of each word and between each word the silent spaces.

It is a lovely way to connect with the depth of a spiritual path! Nourishment for the soul!

Listen to a Spiritual Talk by a True Teacher, Philosopher or Artist

Different spiritual teachers not only say different things, but the quality of each has its own resonance.

I love listening to Osho, Krishnamurti, John de Ruiter, Francis Lucille and A. Ramana, amongst others, and, if I could, I'd listen to Jesus, Simon Bar Yochai, Rabbi Nachman of Breslov, St. Francis, Rumi, Mohammed, Moses, Abraham, Sarah, Basho and Sosan.

Who is on your list?

Finding Hidden Treasures of Sound

The first human voice to be recorded was in 1860. The recording was done as a graph onto smoke blackened paper, which could not be played back, at least not until 2007 when modern technology allowed what was recorded to be converted back into sound and heard again.

The first device to both record and play back music was developed by Thomas Edison and introduced in 1877, although the recording was on a fragile, easily damaged medium. Improvements allowed longer lasting and higher quality recordings to be made. Existing sound recordings of artists go back to 1889 with a recording of what is likely the voice of the great composer, Johannes Brahms.

Because of this technology we can now listen to poets like Walt Whitman, American presidents such as Théodore Rosevelt, the founder of modern nursing, Florence Nightingale, the Russian composer, Peter Tchaikovsky, the great magician, Harry Houdini and many others...

When we hear a voice from the past, it conveys something of the person's inner qualities, their resonance...If that person has something of great value to share, we can absorb something of it – not so much intellectually, but viscerally.

"*In every moment the Universe is whispering to you.*"

Denise Linn,
The Secret
Language of Signs

SUBTLE SOUNDS

Listen to the Whispers, to the Tiniest Sounds

Listen as if you are being whispered a secret you really want to hear, as if you don't want to miss anything!

Buttonbush (*Cephalanthus occidentalis*) flower

Listen to the Subtlest Realms (the Fairy Realm, Trees)

There's a dimension at the edge of light and sound, subtle and elusive, that I call the fairy realm. It's a magical place, accessible when you stop, tune in and listen with a wondering openness.

Listen to the Still Quiet Voice Inside You

The inner voice that guides you and which knows what is right for you does not usually shout. Rather, you "hear" it in stillness, awareness, and presence. At any moment, stop! Listen attentively...

"Not that which goeth into the mouth defileth a man;
but that which cometh out of the mouth,
this defileth a man."

Mathew 15:11

Viceroy (*Limenitis archippus*)

SPEAK CAREFULLY, CONSCIOUSLY

Listen to yourself speaking

Bring awareness to your own speaking. What do you sound like at different times, with different people and different moods. Be aware and vigilantly careful of your words, so that they convey the best of you.

Save any cathartic or negative speech for your private release, but with people and sentient beings speak with the kindest, most centered, presence, as destructive speech lingers and is most difficult to undo! It's very hard to take back or erase harsh words!!!

Different tones reflect how you are feeling inwardly. What's the quality of your voice when you are complaining, whining or being judgmental. What's it like when you are sad, tired, or feeling down? What's your voice like when you are happy or confident?

More then just words, does the quality of your voice bring forth what you wish to share? Do you speak with confidence and clarity. Listening to your own speaking will over time help you to shift limiting patterns of expression. Notice your body positions, your posture and breathing at the same time as the quality of your voice. For example, if you slump when speaking to certain people, you might find this awareness changing your posture.

Simple awareness through listening can be healing and transformative!

"*Meditation is not a separate thing from life; it is the very essence of life, the very essence of daily living. To listen to those bells, to hear the laughter of that peasant as he walks by with his wife, to listen to the sound of the bell on the bicycle of the little girl as she passes by: it is the whole of life, and not just a fragment of it, that meditation opens.*"

J. Krishnamurti, Meditations

HARMONY, SOUND AND SILENCE

Burmese Gong, late 19th century, metal-wood. Source: Metropolitan Museum, New York *Image Public Domain*

Listen to a gong or bells striking and sounds fading

When a gong or bell is struck it is like a Zen master's stick, "Awake, awake."

Let the gong or bell awaken you!

Then listen to the sounds as they fade into silence. Merge into this silence: It is so enjoyable, and easy to move into stillness through a fading sound.

It is amazing how something so simple as following a fading sound into silence can bring us so far into a sense of serenity and peace!

Humming

Humming tunes us, bringing the non-resonating parts of us into harmony. Take time to hum, sit in a quiet spot, lips closed and hum, letting the tone change as it will. Listen as you hum. Give whatever time you can, 20 minutes, 30 minutes or 40 minutes are enough. Sit silently after humming, gently listening.

Grand Piano, 1720, Florence, Italy, made by Bartolomeo Cristofori, who is considered as the inventor of the piano. This is the earliest of three surviving pianos made by Cristofori. Source: Metropolitan Museum, New York
Image Public Domain

TOMSON HIGHWAY – SOME THOUGHTS ON SILENCE

It's great to have as a neighbor one of the finest writers in Canada, perhaps in all of the English or French world. I see Tomson Highway on his bicycle, walking or in his car. He stops and we chat. He is also a playwright, children's author, pianist and composer. He is a master of the Cree language, which he says is rich in humor, French and English, and other languages as well. We talk about art, architecture, our amazing fathers, language and about the silence in the vastness of the North.

I lived in Nunavut, the immense Northern Territory, for 7 years, and have experienced something of its silence. Tomson was born into it and imbibed it throughout childhood. So, I am so glad he agreed to share some of his thoughts on silence that is part of him, his writing and music.

I was born in silence on top of the world in sub-arctic Canada. It is one of the most isolated and thus one of the most beautiful spots on Earth, where meet vast territories, the provinces of Manitoba and Saskatchewan on the one hand and on the other the territories called the Northwest Territories and Nunavut (formed in 1999). The last-named territory alone rivals in size all western Europe from the Russian border to the Atlantic Ocean.

One statistic people are shocked to discover is that the distance from the northern extremity of Canada to the South is only slightly less than the distance from East to West across Canada. The top half of Canada is almost unpeopled. That is where my people live, the great Cree nation.

Not that our region of the world is without life, quite the contrary. No census-taker worth his weight in gold has ever had the wherewithal to make the calculation, but the lakes in Canada are thought to number over two million. By comparison, Holland has few, Spain has two, Australia has thousands, Saudi Arabia has zero, and so go the numbers. And 95% of Canada's water – if one may make a soaring estimate – is still drinkable, still rivals in purity and nutritional value the most expensive of Evian or Perrier water. The fish in those lakes are all uncountable. The birds and the mammal who breathe the air above, the fur-bearing animals who make it their hearth and home, and the small animals thriving beneath tangled bushes, these are not countable, not at all.

Nunavut is the same size as Western Europe which, these days, pushes one billion residents, while Nunavut boasts a mere 39,000.

Where I was born and raised in Northern Manitoba, there was nothing there, no town, no village, no human settlement, one of the most isolated places on Earth. In terms of humans, there was just our family: my parents and what were, at one time, their 11 children of which I am the 11th.

When I was a child we had no electricity, no radios, no noise. But we did not have silence, not in the way most humans know it, because there were the sounds of animal life rich beyond compare. To my father, my mother, my siblings and myself -- all of this, the land, animal life and elements of nature -- was a vast silence.

"The vibrations on the air are the breath of God speaking to man's soul. Music is the language of God."

Ludwig van Beethoven

LISTENING AND SYNCHRONICITY

The sound
of waves.

Photo:
Grant Tigner

Listening attunes us to synchronicity, which I see as the revelation and recognition of an underlying intelligence, harmony and convergence of events in the unfoldment of life.

Synchronicity is God speaking to us.

Listening brings us in tune with the omnipresent, divine intelligence. When we know we are attuned, even for an instant, it is an ah ha! moment of deep wonderous satisfaction!

"Those who have found the Truth have first learned to listen to the Heart, to the "still small voice," to the Holy of Holies within consciousness. The Heart is the place of knowing."

William Samual, A Guide to Awareness and Tranquillity

"When we dance, the journey itself is the point, as when we play music the playing itself is the point. And exactly the same thing is true in meditation. Meditation is the discovery that the point of life is always arrived at in the immediate moment.

Alan Watts

PART 2

RATTLING

THE RATTLE AND RATTLING

A finely made rattle over 4,000 years old from ancient Egypt, 2323–2291 B.C.E. It is known as a sistrum and is inscribed with the name of King Teti. *"A sort of musical rattle, the sistrum was shaken in cadence, marking the rhythm at religious ceremonies. Its soothing music, evoking an ancient rite—the "shaking of the papyrus"—warded off the violence of dangerous deities, Hathor in particular."* Source: Metropolitan Museum, New York *Image Public Domain*

The rattle is a beautiful musical instrument, very basic and primal, found in many forms across cultures and time.

It is given to babies who love a rattle. A baby rattle is universal.

Rattling touches something fundamental in us. When we rattle, it brings us in tune into the greater harmony. It can bring us in tune with the highest vibrations and resonance.

Through rhythmic movement and deep listening, rattling allows us to enter a meditative state of silence and presence.

The sounds of rattling reach into the subtle and elemental, the origins of sound, attuning to the particles of sound and vibration. Rattling may help dissolve disease and blocks, freeing energy.

Rattling can bring us answers to our questions. Ask a question and rattle, the answers come.

Therefore, rattling is a meditation; it is for answers, attuning, alignment and healing. It is to send waves of love and good vibrations. It can be prayerful. It may bring us in tune and harmony with others, our environment and with righteous beings.

Columbian wood
seed rattle, 18th
century.
Source: Metropolitan
Museum, New York
Image Public Domain

Shaken Idiophones or Rattles in an Enclosed Vessel

Rattles belong to a class of instruments known as Shaken
Idiophones (Idiophone is an instrument usually made of
a hard material such as wood or metal that vibrates when
struck or shaken).

Names of various types of rattles include the Cabasa,
Maracas, Rainstick, Rebana, Shekere, Sistrum (when shaken
the small rings or loops of thin metal on its movable crossbars
produce a sound from a soft clank to a loud jangling), Toy
rattles (sometimes used as a Teether, a toy given to soothe an
infant during teething), Tambourine and Timbrel.

In this book, we are primarily engaged with what is perhaps
the most basic form of the rattle, known as a vessel rattle. A
vessel such as a coconut shell, a leather pouch, a gourd or even a
tin can is filled with small objects such as seeds or pebbles that
when shaken strike against each other and the walls of the vessel.

What are the techniques of rattling?

First to consider is that although there are techniques, rattling can be done immediately, spontaneously. And, as we rattle, the techniques of rattling flow naturally.

To start all you need is a basic rattle: a vessel or container, a shell with pebbles, seeds, or other small hard objects and perhaps a handle. If a rattle has a handle, then it is easy to move it with the wrist back and forth making a frapping sound or move it side to side or round and round, fast or very slow... letting the pebbles inside roll. Or you can move the whole arm with your body and then the rattling has a different, more definite sound.

Rattling may be done with either hand or two rattles, one in each hand.. It is good to alternate hands. If you rattle on the right side, then it is good to switch to the left, to create balance between the different sides of our body/mind, of our brain. With two rattles you may also alternate between them, changing tones.

*"The true work of art is but
a shadow of the divine perfection."*

Michelangelo

Raven Rattle 19th
century, Haida Indian,
British Columbia,
Canada.
Source: Metropolitan
Museum, New York
Image Public Domain

WHAT KIND OF RATTLE SHOULD YOU GET?

The rattle used for meditation, alignment, and healing is a sacred object and is treated with reverence and care.

Even the simplest and crudest rattle, even a plastic rattle meant for a baby, absorbs the energy from sacred rituals, rites and meditations. It will carry the energy of the inner work. Take care of it as something of great value.

There are rattle makers who know their craft and the art of creating a rattle for sacred work. Such a rattle may be beautiful to look at, adorned with symbols or designs that connect us to our guides and highest consciousness, and filled with sacred pebbles or seeds that create a resonant, pleasing sound. The rattle maker works prayerfully and blesses the rattle. Such a rattle is truly precious.

If we can make our own rattle, lovingly, carefully, in a prayerful mood, calling upon blessings each step of the way, then such a rattle, even if made from simple objects and materials, carries our personal resonance, our energy signature, and our intentions. It connects us to our inner guidance and is a powerful tool for our personal work, especially as a help to find answers to questions that arise about our life, and actions. At some point, every rattler may eventually wish to make their own rattle or rattles, to add to their collection, for multiple rattles each attuned to a different resonance are beneficial in our work.

SEAN WALKING BEAR – MASTER RATTLE MAKER

I've had the privilege to own and rattle with some of the wonderful rattles made by the master rattle maker, Sean Walking Bear. They are sacred items, lovingly made with conscious intention, true works of art, and they can be used for any of the work described in this book whether meditation, healing, or ritual.

Sean graciously shares the basis of his work and making of rattles in this succinct and highly informative interview.

Who were the rattle makers that preceded you and taught you?

My teachers were local artisans and Medicine Men of the community. Sadly, most have passed away, taking much of their knowledge with them, as apprentices are hard to find in recent generations.

How, when, where were rattles used?

Rattles are used in various ceremonies, rites, gatherings, feasts, prayer, meditation, trances, and in spiritual warfare. Ceremonial use can include sweat lodges, pipe ceremonies, night lodges, and healing sessions.

How far back does the tradition go?

The gift of the rattle may date back to the age of the first people on Earth. I had a vision come to me regarding the rattle I can share. Long ago, the first peoples were found in need of healing, prayer, worship, song, and dance. They were soon pitied by the other beings of the Earth, who then joined together to bless the first Human tribes of the Earth with the gift of the rattle. This gift would come from all Kingdoms of God's Creation. The animal kingdom offered their furs and skins to craft the rattle. The plants and tree kingdom offered their wood for handles and seeds to fill the rattle. Mother Earth offered her rocks to fill the rattle and sand to shape the rattle. The first humans were then taught how to craft and use the rattle; to share with future generations.

Tell us about the learning of rattle making: when did you start learning the craft?

I learned through inspection, observation, inquiry, and curiosity. I was fascinated by shamanic art, as it seemed like magic to me. I wanted to learn the craft and was highly motivated to become an artist myself.

What made you decide to do this work?

I eventually became a devout Medicine Man, committed to walking the righteous path. My skill and knowledge of shamanic art and tools grew exponentially and became a benefit to my own practice. I knew deep inside; I was somehow chosen as an artisan to share my shamanic art and my tools with other spiritual practitioners.

What inwardly did you learn?

I grew up around Medicine Men who would use shamanic tools such as drums and rattles for ceremony and ritual, including spiritual warfare. These tools were essential and were made by artisans skilled in a very particular shamanic art. I was fascinated with the fact you could make something out of anything as an artist. I wanted to learn their craft and would continually ask them questions. Over the years, I became adept at repairing and adding artistic nuances to existing rattles, eagle fans, drums, and artifacts. I would carefully examine their tools almost reverse engineering them to further understand and learn how to craft my own. You quickly learn the 'Tricks of the Trade' and discover each individual artist's techniques and design. Eventually I became an artist in my own right, focusing on Native American art and Shamanic Tools.

What are the qualities of a good rattle?

A good rattle should last generations, outliving each heir, retaining its sound and magic, with minimal repairs necessary related to wear and tear.

What is the process of making a rattle?

I feel answering this question would require writing a book. There is so much involved, as it is an art and science, as well as magic and spirituality. Plus, there are many secrets I would be giving away in the process; save for my apprentices.

What influences and themes do you bring to your designs?

I am influenced by the Shamanic world of magic, spirits, paranormal, spiritual warfare, the Creator, the Earth, and its medicines.

How do you create the sound of each rattle?

Different rattle materials require specific 'fills' to produce an adequate and reasonably audible resonance and vibration. I incorporate a variety of stones, metals, glass, gems, and crystals. Some fills will just not work in some instances, and may sound flat, soft, and muffled; correcting the fill will allow for a perfect sound to be produced. I love to experiment and change the 'fill' to create a variety of sounds. For example, I craft an Autonomous Sensory Meridian Response (ASMR) rattle which produces a very relaxing, rain-like sound, a soothing vibration, with a lower and more tranquil decibel level.

How do you suggest that we take care of a rattle?

Best to keep your hands clean when using and invest in a rattle bag for transport and storage.

What suggestions do you have for those wishing to engage with the rattle in a meaningful way?

Use sincerely. Practice as much as possible. It can be used for prayer, meditation, chanting, ceremony, healing, spiritual warfare, house clearing, and getting into a trance.

STAGES OF RATTLE MAKING

Rattle heads

Assembled rattled

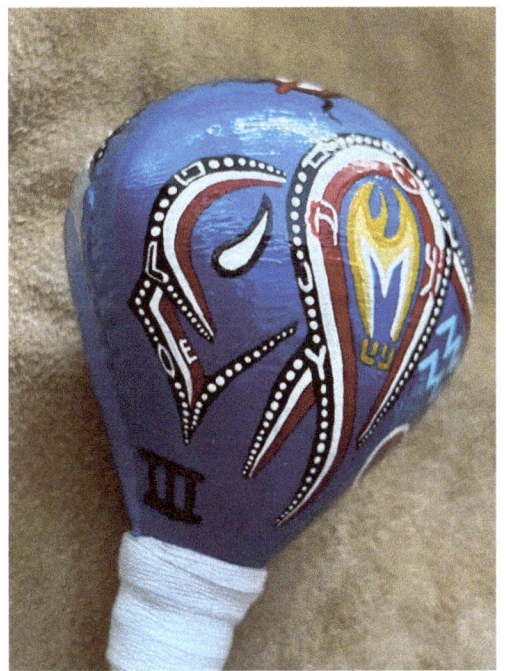

Finished head of rattle

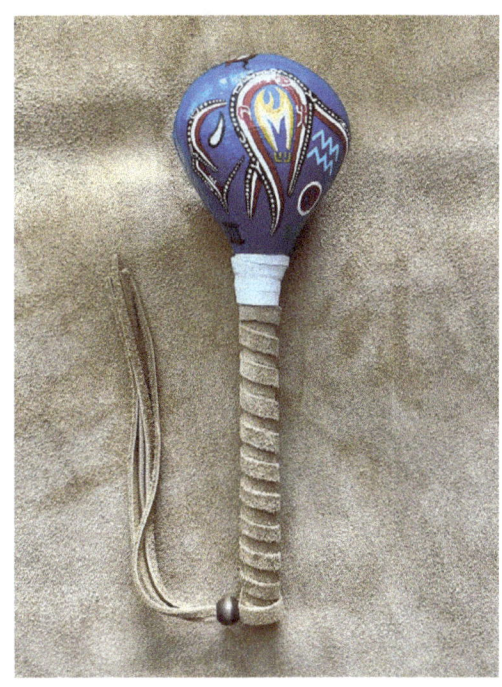

Completed rattle

Sean Mah AKA Sean Walking Bear is a Plains and Woodland Cree Artist, Actor, Author, and Entrepreneur currently based in Las Vegas, NV, USA. Sean was born and raised in a small Cree First Nations/Native American community in Northern Alberta, Canada. Much of his youth was immersed in spirituality, religion, art, shamanism, the paranormal, and magic.

Sean detailing

Medicine Men have always been family and his lifelong teachers, he became an apprentice at a very young age, earning his first pipe by the time he was 18 years old. Sean was fascinated with the fact that communication with the Creator and the heavens was a key part of spirituality and the path of the Shaman—He committed his life to walking a righteous path filled with prayer, ceremony, and spiritual warfare. Another facet of Native American

culture and ceremony is shamanic art; essential tools, often spiritual weapons, practical, and blessed. Sean quickly learned the way of the shamanic artisan, having studied these tools, learning from local artists, and Medicine Men since the early 1990s.

He learned the ancient ways of creating these tools, using prayer, fasting, and ritual. Sean continually hones and perfects his craft, constantly innovating, creating new techniques and tools of the trade—having crafted over 4000 rattles since opening his shop in 2014.

Sean currently shares ceremony and prayer in Las Vegas, NV., including hosting classes based on spirituality and shamanic art. Sean's art can be found on platforms such as Etsy, online stores such as Sunreed, and **www.therattlemaker.com**

*"I haven't understood a bar of music in my life,
but I have felt it."*

Igor Stravinsky

PREPARING YOUR SPACE AND YOURSELF FOR RATTLING

The Seven Directions

Everything said in our description of rattling should be taken as suggestions. Experiment and test out what works for you.

As a preamble to a rattling session, a rite or ceremony, a healing session or meditation, rattle and sing an invocation to each direction such as, "Ayi ee yahh, ayi ee yahh," or a chant of your own choosing.

Start in the East, then South, West, North, the Mother Earth below, the infinite Sky above, and finishing with Within, rattling at the heart.

You may also say a spontaneous prayer in your own words or a prayer that you know that brings forth in you a deeper connection with the Source, a prayer asking for guidance and protection. You may invoke the presence of sacred masters and teachers and of the light and intelligence of the Source, the Great I AM. Your starting invocation creates the right space to begin your inner work, a safe place to open your heart and energy.

Be careful in this inner work, because rattling is a powerful tool, expanding our consciousness. At times we enter the spirit world, another dimension than our normal, solid, familiar framework of reality. Preparing your space, ensuring you remain grounded, is necessary, especially if working alone. If you work with an experienced guide, then he or she may prepare the space, ensuring that the space remains pure and safe for everyone. Then it is easier to let go and move even deeper than when you work alone.

Burn Incense as an Offering

In the Zohar, the Book of Splendour, the great work of Kabbalah - an oral commentary on the Torah that came to be written down to preserve it and make it available to all - it is said that burning incense is a sacred act that is as pleasing to the Creator and as powerful as prayer.

What kind of incense should you burn? The finest natural incense is favoured. Beyond that, find incense with aromas that resonate best with you.

According to the Jewish mystic, Rabbi Nachman (1772 to 1810) of Breslov, in the Ukraine, the Torah requires that the plant called Galbanum be included in any incense formulation. By itself, it is said to have a vile fragrance but adds a note that completes incense.

For purification: Cedar (Thuja), Sage, and Sweetgrass may be used around the room and to purify ourselves.

Spraying vibrational tree and flower essences mixed with essential oils around ourselves and the space is both delightful and an effective mode of purification.

Clothing

When rattling in a group ceremony or when you feel inwardly directed, wear your ceremonial clothes, clothing that, if possible, is used only for meditations and rites.

Natural materials, especially silk and wool absorb the vibrations and hold in the energy.

On your own, in your day-to-day meditations and rites, you may wear your house clothes or rattle naked. Be loose and natural.

Covering yourself in a prayer or meditational shawl blessed by a master or blessed by its having been used in spiritual practice is highly desirable and beneficial. Wearing such a shawl is to envelop yourself in a higher energy that can protect and open your psyche. In many spiritual paths, the disciple meditates on the tomb or Samadhi of an awakened being, a master, a righteous person or a sage. Placing a shawl on a tomb with the intention of absorbing the energy presence, the resonance of the being, will imbue the material vibrationally with that sacred presence as well as connect you emotionally and spiritually with the path.

"... Frequently, the dancers themselves handle the rattles, each carrying one in his hand and shaking it as he steps. Used in this way the rattle is an inspiration to the dancer, its rattling sound serving as a constant incentive to perform, and moreover, it serves as an aid to rhythmic movement—it seems to make possible the achievement of all movements in harmony with the rhythm with less effort.

From *How to Make Drums, Tomtoms & Rattles*, by Bernard S. Mason

RATTLING AND INSPIRATION

Dance

Let the energy flow. Blocked energy brings physical and psychic stagnation and even illness. Rattling helps open our energy flow.

Flowing energy is one of the keys for a fruitful spiritual practice. When we flow, we connect with life, love and laughter and allow the divine source to have direction over our life.

It's wonderful to rattle and dance. Just dance and let go. Allow this time to be without any goal, without anything to be accomplished.

Creativity

How can rattling support our creativity?

Creativity is birthed in the rich dark soil of our inner being, "Creatio ex nihilo (Latin for 'creation out of nothing')" You come closest to this in deep sleep, deep meditation - moments of let go. Rattling can lead us into that state.

You may feel sleepy after a longer rattling session. If it is so, and your wish is to open creative channels, then after rattling, it is good to rest—even sleep. That sleep may be silent and full of grace. In deep sleep with awareness, you may receive the gift of experiencing the ground of creativity and being.

Artist Grant Tigner, the author's father, painting in Yellowstone National Park, 1996.

Beyond general indications: specific rattling exercises may be done for different creative avenues such as hands-on crafts, visual creation, music, dance and movement. Through rattling you can access different parts of our creative vehicle, of the creative process. The key is to adapt the rattling to the creative medium you are exploring. For Dance, dance while rattling; for Music, rattle, sing and listen to music; for Writing, rattle and then jot down your words – likewise for other arts, rattle and then take a creative step.

Rattling focuses our creative energy in the direction we desire. Our intuition flows. The feeling may be subtle. Be attentive and confident, because there are no mistakes here. If the creative act doesn't seem to flow, rattle gently again. If need be, be patient, leave everything aside, don't force things.

Dreamwork

You may enter creative dreams, especially if in your rattling you have invoked a creative project or process or asked a question, then the dreams will turn around that process or question.

Before bedtime rattle while holding to the intention that your dreaming will reveal something related to a question or theme that are the subject of your creativity. One way that you may suddenly know while dreaming that you are in the dream world is to remember yourself rattling, or to see an image of your rattle. If your rattle is painted with a beautiful image, all the more effective to recall it during sleep (The rattle I would use for such work, created by Sean Walking Bear, is painted with a blue butterfly and is attuned in sound to the 3rd eye – perfect for dreamwork).

Awareness in a dream may not happen right away, but if you persist with rattling for 10 to 15 minutes each night with a clear intention, one night in a flash you may see yourself in a dream body rattling, or you may see your rattle, or you may simply find yourself aware.

Keep a Journal for Creative Flashes and Noting Dreams

Aside from rattling, it is helpful in dreamwork and creativity to keep a journal. Creative flashes come out of nowhere, momentarily illuminating your path. We have all had the experience of a brilliant idea arising suddenly and then disappearing. Try to get things down in your journal before they disappear from your consciousness, later becoming difficult to retrieve. Likewise, write down your dreams before they disappear from memory.

Copper rattle and stone head, thought to be 3rd to 10th century, Peru. Source: Metropolitan Museum, New York
Image Public Domain

Rattling in Nature

No better place is there to rattle than outdoors in nature. Rattle to fall in tune with the trees and grasses, rocks and streams, flowers and birds, butterflies and bees, the clouds and the sky, the air and the sun and stars.

Rattling at night brings us into the mystery and we feel like the stars are our sister and brothers. Rattling, wish upon a star, and take the star's energy into your belly.

In the daytime, be in tune with the light of the sun; let it warm your being, bathe in this blessing!

Rattle until you feel yourself merging with nature, with the life around you and the mother earth.

You may obtain a deep silent communion. That is a great gift to body, mind and soul!

You may talk to God, the omnipresent divine intelligence, or to a spiritual mentor or master or even a beloved ancestor or elder.

All of this becomes easy when rattling in nature.

Breathe deeply and easily, naturally as you rattle.

Let your prayers be carried by the trees and grasses. They will help you and speak with you, sending your prayers to every nook and corner, the earth and sky, the visible realm and the invisible realm.

Take your time. When the rattling is complete, sit or lie on the earth. Ground yourself. Above all, express your gratitude in words, songs or silence, being sure to fully take in and absorb the experience.

*"Live this moment. Live it intensely, totally,
passionately, and then a Miracle happens."*

Osho, note to author

Bes Rattle, Egyptian Faience (a process of glazing ceramics), Egypt, circa 945-664 BCE. The image in the rattle is of a beneficent domestic god. "The Bes-rattle must have been used in a ritual performance, and Bes's known role as a protector of women and childbirth suggests the rituals addressed such concerns."
Source: Metropolitan Museum, New York
Image Public Domain

SOUL WORK

Rattling and Trance States

Rattling naturally induces altered states. In meditation, we wish to hold a double-edged awareness: awareness of Self – of being conscious of being conscious – and, at the same time, attentive to what is arising before us, for example, listening attentively to the sounds of the rattle. It is often helpful to vary the rhythm and strength of the rattling to help us remain alert.

A rhythmic sound may also induce a trance state, which is desirable in Shamanic journeying where we need to let go of control and be carried into the spirit realm. The rattler will maintain a steady rhythm, timed in synch with the beating of the heart. This will induce a soothing trance as well, and if it is a group process, bring all participants into a shared trance that amplifies and carries the work of the group. At the end of the session, the rhythm is increased, and the trance is broken. It is best to take it step by step, gently making changes, bringing you back to a normal waking state, grounded and present in the body and alert to the world around you.

In a rattling session intended to alter our mind frame or thought patterns, a hypnotic or trance state may facilitate the work of the hypnotist, whose core work is really a sort of de-hypnosis, freeing us from limiting or negative mental habits. Here the rhythm may follow the intention of the work, being rhythmic to induce and deepen entry into trance, but when an undesired thought pattern is being uprooted, the rattling can change to a more shaking kind of sound, supporting the release process. If after cleansing unwanted patterns we wish to embed new and more positive and beneficial thought patterns, then a soft, gentle rhythm may be followed. For best results, the key is for the rattler to remain carefully attuned to the subject and the progress of the session, to let the rattling follow the current or stream, so to speak.

How Can Rattling Connect You to the Source?

The universe, the All, is interpenetrated with the spirit of intelligence. Ungraspable, it is called by many names, but there are no words to express it. All is in the hands of this divine intelligence.

We rattle to affirm our recognition of the Source of All. That is the highest dimension of rattling.

There is no how to, but there are certain attitudes that are keys to entering this state of consciousness, such as maintaining an inner attitude of prayer.

Any time, day or night, pick up your rattle and call to this mysterious intelligence. Sing and dance.

Rattling as Meditation

Alternatively, rather than focusing on insights that arise, contemplating or reflecting on what presents itself, you may choose to take a meditative approach, which means to be in silent awareness as you rattle, simply witnessing any thoughts and emotions. Sit (or stand) in a position that helps you maintain alertness, deliberately putting aside thinking, that is, choosing not to indulge in thoughts, no matter how fascinating, alluring, significant or insightful they may seem.

However, thoughts will arise naturally and take you with them: one moment you are alert, the next you find your self in a dreamlike thought sequence. What should you do then? Be gentle and kind to yourself! Allow awareness to be easy and unforced. You wish to maintain an even attitude, remaining neutral to thoughts that arise, neither indulging in thinking nor struggling or fighting with thoughts. Therefore, when you catch yourself in a dreamlike sequence, simply note it and let it go.

Veracruz, Mexico, 600-1,000 C.E., smiling figure
Source: Metropolitan Museum, New York
Image Public Domain

How Long Can You Rattle?

You may rattle for as short a time as a few seconds... Or you may rattle for ten minutes, 20 minutes, forty minutes or longer.

Rattling can begin and end a meditation or healing session.

If you have something inside you that needs attention such as an inner strong movement of memory/emotions, a need for resolving an inner dilemma or conflict, then rattling can be done until something shifts in your psyche. The key in determining the length of time is to allow the rattling to complete itself. Let rattling come to its own conclusion and then rattle a little longer focusing on coming back to your present environment, awareness of your body, sensations and emotions. This way you will return from the session feeling grounded. Be gentle with yourself after a session. If need be, rest to absorb the effects of the process.

Cog Rattle, France, 15th century
used in the Catholic Church for the celebration of Mass during Holy Week (the week before Easter and the last part of Lent)
Source: Metropolitan Museum, New York
Image Public Domain

Rattling can have a fixed time as in a daily meditation.

The keeping of chronological - linear time by the calendar and clock - allows us to keep agreements, to order our lives in sync with our community, and to function effectively in the world. Schedules and timeframes are needed to create an efficient, technological world where we live in comfort and abundance with food, shelter and other resources readily available.

But in contrast and opposition to clock time, there are the uncounted time of the rhythms in nature, the psychological time governed by our emotional needs, and the spiritual, vertical, non-linear time that is experienced when the thinking mind is silent, and a sense of wonder and awe opens us to the undefined and eternal.

If we listen to the beat of the rattle attentively, we lose track of linear time and enter the timeless. Even if you have a timeframe for a rattling session, within that time, your wish is to let go into the timeless. But nothing can be forced. Letting go is a knack, it cannot be commanded; rather you slip into it.

One obstacle to our inner work is the feeling of impatience, which can come from the habit of watching the clock. Have you noticed that even when you have gotten somewhere you have desired to be, you may still look at the clock, wanting to get somewhere else, to advance to something different. From force of habit, clock time has become entrained in our psyches, and we compulsively track it. Thereby, while rattling, impatience may arise, and this may happen frequently in the beginning. Rather than becoming frustrated, you will find it beneficial to adopt an attitude of patience with your impatience. Simply continue to rattle, let the feeling of impatience arise and subside on its own, then rattling can take you into moments of silent freedom.

Terracotta rattles, Cypriot, 1600 to 1450 B.C.
Source: Metropolitan Museum, New York
Image Public Domain

How Can Rattling Be Incorporated into a Spiritual Practice?

A spiritual practice is an attitude that feels the sacredness of life: it is an integral part of how you live. In a spiritual practice, awareness of being and a reverence for the mystery have become primary: the ups and downs, successes and failures, and challenges and delights of the world are now recognized as being secondary, because, like quicksand, they are ever changing. Still, you remain capable of acting, but your actions have begun to reflect your inner spiritual practice.

Life is celebrated in all its dimensions and spirit is exalted.

Rattling – music and dance – are a bridge from the visible to the invisible. Let the rattle shake, it is a dance. Let your whole body move with this dance. Let the mind be absorbed in the primal sounds and allow thoughts to slow down. Let yourself be empty and dissolve into the emptiness.

In a spiritual practice it is not what you believe which is primary, but the silent flow of energy. A witnessing consciousness, awareness of the source, and flowing energy bring delight, release, and one day, transcendental awakening, and luminosity!

A rattle is a tool – primal, an extension of your own hands and body. Use it, enjoy it, love it and one day drop it, because it is not an end in and of itself.

If, as part of your spiritual work you practice rattling, the rewards are many and great.

Meditation for Couples and Groups

Rattling is a good meditation for couples because it brings harmony and alignment. Rattle together. Synchronize your rattling and movements. Look into each others' eyes. As you rattle and move together, you begin to resonate together like cords in a guitar, you fall in tune.

A group rattling session can take us into a wondrous state of meditative awareness, bringing a tangible sense of transcendental oneness. It can facilitate profound healing.

If people participate by rattling around someone sitting, standing or lying in the middle, each covering one of the four directions, they bring powerful healing forces to bear.

Crocodile Rattle, Mayan, ceramic, 8th century, Mexico. It functions both as a whistle (it has air holes on the underside of its legs), and a rattle (it has clay pellets in the front) and is painted with a bright color known as Mayan indigo.
Source: Metropolitan Museum, New York
Image Public Domain

Spontaneous Rattling Meditation

At any time, suddenly stop and take a few minutes to rattle, listen and become more and more present.

Also, whenever possible, take advantage of key moments of the day, when ever there is a gap in between activities or changing states. For example, upon waking or before falling into sleep it is propitious to rattle, as the awareness awakened, and the tone will continue through the day or night.

Deep in the Night

The depth of night (midnight to 3 or 4 am) –when all is quiet, and the business and busyness of the day has receded – is a magical time. The sacred presence is tangible. We may speak and converse with words and prayers or silence. At this delicate hour, rattle softly as if the rattling is your prayer and you will feel joined to the Great Source.

UNMANI LENGER ON RATTLING,
SOUL AND SHAMANIC WORK

Unmani is a very loving and courageous Soul Worker who in the following interview tells us about her many years of experience of rattling and the many dimensions of soul and shamanic work. I am most grateful for her sharing her insights and wisdom.

Shamanic Work and Rattling

Could you tell us about your shamanic work over the years?

You can't speak about shamanic work without mentioning a rattle or a drum, because the basic shamanic work is about divination. You have a question, and you want to ask the question to somebody who maybe knows more than you do. And then you use your rattle or your drum to access realms beyond the everyday consciousness.

I rattle most times when people come. I rattle and I go to power animals or a teacher. You can also journey to beings in the middle world to explore your question.

Rattling is a very important thing in this work, although, which I find very interesting, I did things with Celtic shamanic work, and they also do journey sometimes without a rattle. I didn't know that. I did some studies with Tom Cowan, who wrote the book *Fire in the Head*. I was surprised at one point that I felt like, aha, how did they do things? And it seems like they journeyed with the rattle, but maybe also without a rattle in a special way. It seems you always need a special way to go.

For instance, you use your rattle or drum, or you take certain body postures, and then you go. It seems that the Celts journeyed by just taking one posture for journeying.

I've explored a lot. I'm very keen on possibilities. I love to go deeper with things.

Pre-Columbian Rattle,
100 BCE - 200 CE,
Jalisco, Mexico
Terracotta with kaolin
(soft clay)
The rattle is concealed
behind the nursing
female figure.
Source: Metropolitan
Museum, New York
Image Public Domain

Divination and Soul Retrieval

The shamanic work is a lot about this divination work, but it's also a lot about soul retrieval. It is a beautiful work: many shamans all over the world think that if you have had traumatic experiences, parts of your soul leave for you to be able to stay. If part of the soul leaves, you stay, but you don't feel whole, yet that's better than to not be there. You stay yet you miss something: we all know that feeling we're missing something.

In soul retrieval, we have a look at which parts have left, and which parts are ready to come home again. You use a rattle to journey to get the part back and to make it stay with you.

In that work a rattle is definitely helpful. You could do it with a drum, yet I find the rattle is easier to handle.

First you go and you look for those pieces. Once you get them, then you put them into the bodies of the people again. For them to be able to stay, you go and rattle around the person.

The rattle is very useful, very helpful in that work.

I'm interested in souls. I'm not interested in this or that. If somebody comes, I'm only interested in what this soul is telling, what's needed right now. And we look for the next step.

Quite often it's soul retrieval or it's divination work.

I like when people come with some kind of question in themselves. We go with the question, and we check it out. What's the core of this feeling, what this person really wants. It might be a journey itself where you get answers from the power animal or teacher you're connected with.

There is always something for people to do. You have to integrate information and messages. Or you go for soul retrieval. You go and get the pieces and put them back, get them back home.

And then there's again a time for integration. People must do their own work.

Streaming and Kids

I wanted to ask you also about the work you have done with Streaming (which is a powerful type of energy-healing work, which according to its spirit source, originated in ancient Polynesia)

Streaming is work for women. There is also some work for men, but I did it with women. It's about getting access to the female stream inside the body, which is connected to the earth. Put it like this, you connect to the earth, and your female streamlines, you take this stream from the earth into your breasts and from the breasts, into your arms and hands, and then you lay your hands upon somebody, different parts of the body.

You are led to the right parts. And then you stream this energy into this body, this earth healing energy you make available for the person who needs it.

I haven't used rattling in that work. Streaming is to me a very silent work. It's as if the earth itself offers her gifts. You are in the depth of the earth and through the body, through this allowance, this body stream, you let yourself be "flown." The energy moves through your body. You are as a cup. The energy fills you and you just put out your hands to let it move.

I led circles with training times when you learned it, and practicing times just to use it.

What was very interesting to me was that women loved to use it with their kids. It was more an everyday life practice. When their child needed something, the women would just lay their hands on them. Kids would ask for it, because they knew that their mother had a certain something to offer, which they really loved. This was a big one.

I use everything with my daughter. If there is something she needs, she says, "Mom, please, would you journey for me? In other words, would you please do shamanic work to see closer to an issue?

I think that kids love it if their mothers have certain possibilities to offer, because it's so nice to know I can ask my mom and then she can do this or that and everything works and it's going to be better afterwards.

Water Blessing Ceremony

I wanted to ask you about doing a water blessing or ceremony and about the use of a rattle in that process.

The rattle is important, I need the rattle for that work. To be with all the beings who want to take part in such a ceremony, you need to call them. I use the rattle and call upon all the energies, the beings who are there to support or to just take part.

It's a ceremony for women. There are always women who see colors and beings. They tell tremendously beautiful stories, which colors, which beings they see. In all it is a three-day water ceremony by a river. There are also some women coming the day before who just want to have a talk or connect.

In this water ceremony, there are certain elements which must be there. You call on the spirits and all beings for which you use the rattle. When saying goodbye, it's the same, you use the rattle. The ceremony is always done in a specific way.

Sitting together, the social part is also important. The next day after the ceremony, I just go home.

It's simple. It takes a little bit of time, because people want to speak and to pass on their experience.

The water ceremony is always combined with a certain song, Nee Bee Wah Bow, which is now not the secret song as perhaps it used to be, because there were women who made it available on some social media. Some women liked this, and some didn't, but everything is available on every kind of social media. There are more and more people who are not keen on that. They're not so happy.

Nevertheless, it's like that. It's still a sacred song, so it doesn't change that.

We use wooden sticks for the beat of the song. And after the ceremony, we share the water and then we take some home with us.

The water blessing is something very special. We love it.

Rattling for Another Person

The main thing about rattling for people is the simple fact that there is somebody ready to rattle for you. This itself seems to be a huge-healing thing; people are touched by this. I'm doing this thing in a way that is usual for me, but for people it's unusual. They see me the first time and I say, "You know we could do some shamanic work." When they say, "yes." I say, "Okay, you lie down, and I'll lie beside you. I mean completely unknown people to each other.

So, we lie there, I do it in a certain way, and then I say, "I'm going to rattle."

I feel, and people tell me, that the simple fact that I'm going to rattle is so touching. One of my teachers, Sandra Ingerman, who has written many books about shamanic work, also shared that in her experience the journeying itself is so touching for people, that somebody takes your thing and goes somewhere with this whole thing outside of this everyday life circumstances to bring back healing and wisdom.

Money and Soul Sessions

I have a question that people might struggle with and of course most healers struggle if you're doing a formal session with someone. There is always the question how to share, especially around money. How do you deal with the money thing?

The money thing is interesting. I did a lot of experimenting of different ways to deal with money: I wouldn't ask for anything or I'd asked for something. I'd say, "Do your own way of giving, what you feel you want to give." Or I'd put a range from there to there. I tried many things and where did I end, and I'm still there now, is to put a certain amount. I ask for this amount and put the sentence behind, "If this is possible for you." This works best because in my experience we are so trained with this whole money thing, we are so completely crazy with this whole money thing, that you must get things cheap. If you don't give anything it's better than if you give something.

I feel we are completely polluted with this whole thing about money. It seems to work best if I say, "You know this is the amount that is okay, but if it's not possible for you, if you give less that's okay too."

For groups I do a range thing from there to there. They give what they want. And for certain things, I don't ask for a specific amount, "You give what you want to give."

There is one thing I've found. There are certain people who are wanting to have something done on one hand, but on the other hand they don't want to invest into themselves. They don't want to give anything into that. It's not about money, actually, but it shows in the money issue.

If somebody calls and I hear that she really is not sure what she wants to go for, then I ask for more. Then I'm specific, I say it's this amount, and this is higher than my usual amount. I think that's beautiful because this is the point where they really have to think, "Do I want to have that done, do I really want to go for that?" The money always helps. If it's this amount to me that doesn't really matter this way or that, but it's useful because I don't want to have anybody here at my place who says, "I'll just check it, try it, it might be good or not." I'm not interested. I don't want to waste my time. I'll sit in the sun and have fun, it's better than doing stupid work that is useless. I have though always nice work to do because people decided to go for their thing.

Rattling for Connection

Rattling to me is a lot about making a connection to places, to plants, to trees, to beings, to animals.

Rattling is a beautiful way to connect to some beings, for instance with a plant or with a stone. Usually there are spirits around plants, stones, trees and places. When I stay in nature for some days, I like to rattle for the beings who protect the place. I ask for allowance to be there. I ask for protection and to be with the beings there.

Do you find when you connect using the rattle that those beings respond and also do something like rattling from their side?

It's an interesting question. Maybe this is something about how one's antennas are. I don't hear them rattling. I hear them laughing and speaking and making fun and jokes and protecting and all those things. Yet I haven't heard them rattling. So maybe I'll ask them next time.

Rattling and Clearing Spaces

There are people who ask me for clearing their houses, for cleaning their spaces. The rattle is so important there, for connecting with those beings of ancient times, especially those beings who usually have some serious things that don't allow them to move on. They are dead, they've passed, but they can't see a way to move on. The rattle is important to help them to move on.

What you're saying in a sense is, or at least as I would understand it, is that when you rattle it connects with beings in other dimensions, they're aware of your rattling and it opens a door of communication or even communion?

It's about communicating, and for souls who don't have a body, they often do not know that they don't have a body anymore, so there needs to be some talk about this fact. It needs to be clear that there is a way for them and the rattle is a is an important tool in this whole work.

When a being becomes aware that they're no longer in a body and the need to move on, what happens from your perception? With your rattling, do you connect them with other beings that are say more conscious on that side that can help them move on?

No. It's like they sit in the car and then they are moved on.

You must do the work before so that they are ready to move on. It's just important for them to know they don't have a body anymore, which is by far not clear to many, many beings. Next is to say that there is a way to move on, because usually they feel so imprisoned in something, they don't even exactly know in what. They are here yet nobody knows them, they are here but they are not recognized, they are here they don't know a way out, they are traumatized, and they don't know what to do.

So, if there is somebody who comes and sees them, that's the first thing. The next thing is to be clear about their situation. And next is this longing to go home. This longing is in all of us, I think.

Usually, it takes a little bit of work with these souls, but that's okay. As soon as it's clear that you do this work, lines of souls come, and all want to go on this bridge. Many, many, many come. There were years when I said, "You know, I don't do anything right now, but on Tuesday at three o'clock in the afternoon you can come, and I'll do the whole bunch at once." Otherwise, I would have gone crazy, because so many came. This worked quite well. There were souls lined up wanting to just cross the bridge. It's very touching. There is important work to do on this planet, I feel quite honored to be in this.

Rattling and Consciousness

I would like to add that you can speak about rattling or not rattling or whatever, but the basic thing for me is about consciousness. It's about consciousness, to be conscious that that we are much bigger than we think we are. It's our work to push our own boxes we used to put ourselves into, to push our own limits.

To me it's really about love, love to the earth, to the sky, to all beings, also love to myself, and to make myself available for serving here on this planet. One beautiful way to make myself available is to drum and to rattle for people so that their lives can unfold and be more beautiful and lighter and more conscious than they were. To me that's at the root of the whole rattling thing, but to be honest, it's of course at the root of other things too. It's simple, it's to love and to make yourself available for life.

"Life is a celebration. Consider everything that makes you happy as a gift from God and say, ...'Thank you.'"

— Francis Lucille

Harness Jingle with Stag, 7th – 6th century BCE, China, bronze.
Source: Metropolitan Museum, New York
Image Public Domain

HEALING

What are the healing benefits and other rewards of rattling?

Rattling is one of the most primal and basic forms of sound therapy. In a way it brings us to a level of pre-sound, to the very minutest energy particles in sound, its elemental components. At the most basic level there is emptiness, out of which creation emerges.

Disease is a kind of crystallized chaos, a solidified disharmony. Rattling helps break this up. Then sound energy can be reordered into harmonious, flowing waves. Health then follows.

Because rattling works at such a basic level, it prepares the ground for additional types of vibrational work in sound therapy and other modalities such as tree and flower vibrational essences, light and color therapy and so on. Humming, singing, and other voice work becomes extremely effective after rattling has begun to dissolve and free the solidified energy. In disease there is dissonance, while in health we vibrate in a fuller and more harmonious way.

Rattling has great power in self-healing, healing work on an individual by a healer and in-group healing. Two to seven people rattling around one person is extremely potent. Before rattling around a person, the group should be in sync and their energy clear. It is naturally best to prepare such a session first with meditation and prayer.

If someone feels disturbed, unclear, heavy or in any way challenged by negative sentiments, then it is best to sit aside and not participate in rattling around someone who has requested healing and who is both fragile, open and receptive to the energies of the people who will be rattling.

As well as rattling around an individual, rattling is very effective around a couple experiencing conflict. The couple may sit or stand spine-to-spine or even face-to-face during the rattling (They may then hold hands and look gently into each other's eyes).

Rattling is a very fine tool in preventative health, working at many levels: dissolving the thought forms that are at the start of disease before anything is visible, at the pre-manifestation level.

Rattling Helps Break Down Solidified Patterns

Dis-ease or dis-harmony is often characterized by fixed patterns and stagnant, blocked energy. Rattling brings energy, loosens and breaks up these patterns. Followed by gentle rattling, singing and humming, unhealthy patterns are transformed: disease is dissolved. Using homeopathy, and tree, gem and flower vibrational essences following a rattling session amplifies the healing support of both the rattling and these healing agents. The effects of acupuncture, qigong, tai chi and other energy unblocking processes are also amplified, working hand in hand with rattling.

Rattling Helps Us Channel Healing Forces

You can rattle for yourself, channelling healing forces where needed. Simply remain conscious of where healing in you is needed and rattle until you feel the energy moving there, the area bathed in light and wellness.

Likewise, you may rattle, bringing your awareness to the area of the body or mind of someone you wish to support in healing. When you are most deeply attuned, you will feel in those moments you are in the person you wish to support, or even that you are them. You will feel the flow of light increasing and that part of the person's vehicle in need of support will feel nourished and healing forces beginning to catalyze.

Male northern cardinal
(*Cardinalis cardinalis*)

Our Energy Is Harmonized

When we rattle or listen to rattling together a natural synchronization happens. No special effort other than simply being open and present is needed. Whatever we focus on we harmonize with, begin to resonate with...

Our Thoughts Are Realigned

As thought patterns dissolve into their pre-thought constituents during rattling, you lessen the force of invasive thoughts that pop up and seem to be constantly intruding on your inner sanctum. If you furthermore align to the sacred, thought energies form out of the sacred. It is such a pleasant release from negative and unwanted thoughts.

Rattling Brings Insights and Answers We Need

Rattling opens the doors of perception, allowing you to access different perspectives. In a state of unstructured mind, inner silence or no mind, insights arise depending on where you focus your attention. This is especially valuable if you focus on a source of higher consciousness, a sage, or master, because you are opening windows to the super consciousness.

Clarity comes when the mind is silent, and everything is allowed to sort itself out. While you rattle, be attentive to the act of rattling, the underlying emotions, the mood, the sound of the rattle. Be in a state of active waiting. Confusion may be there, you may feel you are in a cloud, and impatience may be there. Simply rattle without any demands, waiting attentively, and then the fog is lifted.

Spending Conscious Time in Your Own Company Is a Gift

Rattling - going nowhere else but remaining in the moment, spending time with your Self, is to honour and respect yourself. If you can appreciate your Self no matter what may arise as an inner movie, scenario, dream or impulse, this will heal doubts about your worthiness. One way to see it is that you simply are a consciousness, neither worthy nor unworthy.

Rattling Directs and Amplifies the Power of Light and Prayer

Rattling in its purest form is a prayer directing our consciousness to the source. What ever we give attention to grows, expands. This is one of the laws of resonance. As we rattle with consciousness of the source, we direct and amplify the light of the source into our lives.

Horned Rattle, 300 BCE – 200 century CE, Thailand, bronze. Source: Metropolitan Museum, New York *Image Public Domain*

Listening to the Rattle Stops Thoughts

Rattles are given to babies as teethers or pacifiers, to absorb their attention and soothe away discomfort. Listening to rattling, our inner child is nourished. When we give a little attention to the sounds of rattling, thoughts slow down and stop. Then we are freed for a time from the burden of thinking and over time we gain release from invasive and unwanted thoughts that tend to occupy us incessantly.

Rattling to Open and Align our Chakras

Picture your chakras as vortices, spinning energy. Each chakra interacts with an area of the physical body, through the nervous system.

Sound, light, colors, crystal energy work, tree and flower essences and so on affect both the flow and quality of the energy in our chakras. Rattling works on the level of sound and vibration to open, energize, clear, and heal the chakras.

Rattles can be fine-tuned to resonate with a particular chakra, such as the heart, third eye or base, but any rattle can be used to rattle in front or at the back of the body at the location of the chakra.

Each centre is a source point of life affirming energy. The direct vibration and direct attention given to a chakra will resonate there. The power at the sex centre empowers you to connect and express through intimacy, expanding to love, expanding to a consciousness of the whole.

Rattling can be used in conjunction with other chakra work, for example using specific colors directed onto the chakra, or sound or music associated with a chakra. You can sing or chant sounds or a mantra associated with a chakra.

Face Rattle, mid 19th century, from wood, fiber and leather, Tsimshian culture, British Columbia, Canada.
Source: Metropolitan Museum, New York
Image Public Domain

Rattling for Auric Protection

Rattle to clear and strengthen your aura. If we are open — moving into meditation and soul work — but at the same time moving into the world, we may be especially vulnerable to the heavy, stressful, chaotic energies around us.

Aura clearing and building exercises may be necessary and helpful. Rattle with the conscious intention of clearing and filling the aura with light, love, strength. Rattle each day feeling your strength growing. After a session shower or bathe to clear the energies being uprooted.

Along with rattling, protective stones, smudging with cedar, sweet grass or sage, taking vibrational flower and tree essences, are all tools that can help us.

Love and Forgiveness

Loving your Self, your Essence, your Being is fundamental – it is the starting point of love.

You arise from the source of all and return there one day. Loving yourself is therefore to love the source, which is to love all people, plants, animals, rocks and stones, the moon, planets and sun!

Hug yourself when listening to rattling and feel love surrounding you; then without effort, spontaneously send out love.

Forgiveness: Let things that need forgiving arise and let go, consciously forgiving and releasing, whether it is you who wishes forgiveness or it concerns the actions of someone else.

Beaker with Rattle,
900 – 1100 CE, Peru,
gold. Turquoise, resin.
Source: Metropolitan
Museum, New York
Image Public Domain

Singing Someone's Name

Rattle and sing people's names.

It is surprising how powerful it is to sing someone's name with love. It may send shivers of thrills through the person and warm their heart.

In a healing session sing someone's name when they feel open and receptive. It may open the gates of healing, bringing a deep release and resolution of a past wound.

If the person has a name they feel disconnected from, but it is a name that fits with their soul, singing it can help them welcome and integrate their name inside themselves. The person may as a result feel more whole, complete, confident and unified.

If someone feels a need for a new name, then rattling and singing different names may help them discover the names and sounds that bring them joy and satisfaction. They can discover the name that feels right.

*"No matter what is going on,
the background is total peace."*

Stuart Schwartz

RATTLING TO DISSOLVE DISTURBING THOUGHTS AND ENERGIES

Ivory Rattle, 18th –
19th century, Yoruba
peoples, Nigeria.
Source: Metropolitan
Museum, New York
Image Public Domain

Facing and Loosening Inner Disturbances

Heavy, negative and chaotic emotions, thoughts, imprints, desires and tendencies being carried in our psyches need to be released on the spiritual journey. Repressing undesirable elements and forces that arise does not work, except on a temporary basis, as nothing is resolved. What we reject and condemn and try to repress only gives energy to them. Hidden, these elements and forces act in insidious and destructive ways, undermining our well-being, sabotaging our actions, and preventing us from hearing our truth.

At the same time, be aware to not indulge in dreamy and unconscious actions, acting out negative scenarios and amplifying the negative and chaotic in us.

To face disturbing or unwanted emotions, thoughts, imprints, desires and tendencies, consciously allow them to arise while rattling. Feel them as totally as you can moment to moment, being present to them, while at the same time listening to the sound of the rattle. The beat and rhythm of rattling may mirror the elements and forces arising. Allow this. It may help to use your voice to make sounds or speak gibberish. Stay with it until you feel a release, until there is a sense of transcending any disturbing emotions, or simply you feel it is enough for the moment.

As all these disturbing emotions, thoughts, imprints, desires and tendencies are, like physical illness, solidified patterns; the rattling will loosen and then dissolve them.

As in all processes of rattling and other spiritual work, be gentle, sensitive and patient with yourself. There is no need to push yourself too far. Listen to yourself, to your needs. If you have any mental wellness issues, then be especially respectful. Let the rattling be especially light and gentle.

Release as You Rattle

Why don't we have the power to just wish thoughts away? How can we release ourselves from their seeming power over us? If your thoughts go on and on, stubbornly embedded, frustratingly persistent like a broken record, there are ways to release and be free.

Try this mode of catharsis while rattling: Speak your mind in your language, or speak nonsense gibberish, or make faces and releasing sounds. At the same time rattle and wag your tongue from time to time.

The tongue is connected with thinking. When we formulate word thoughts in our mind, the tongue subtly pronounces them.

Try this for 5 minutes each day for a week, followed by 10 minutes, 15 minutes and then 20 minutes in the 4th week, then remain at 20 minutes, no need to extend longer a session.

Follow each release session with an equal time of silence and stillness.

By the end of the 5th or 6th week, you will notice that thought patterns are dissolving and are being released. If you think of thought patterns as recordings like grooves in a record, think of this process as erasing the grooves. Thoughts in grooves keep wanting to repeat themselves, just the right switch and they play themselves in your mind. Releasing these recordings gives you much more inner freedom. Use this time to deepen your silence and to live each moment in its totality.

"The gift of the rattle may date back to the age of the first people on Earth. I had a vision come to me regarding the rattle I can share. Long ago, the first peoples were found in need of healing, prayer, worship, song, and dance. They were soon pitied by the other beings of the Earth, who then joined together to bless the first Human tribes of the Earth with the gift of the rattle. This gift would come from all Kingdoms of God's Creation. The animal kingdom offered their furs and skins to craft the rattle. The plants and tree kingdom offered their wood for handles and seeds to fill the rattle. Mother Earth offered her rocks to fill the rattle and sand to shape the rattle. The first humans were then taught how to craft and use the rattle; to share with future generations."

Sean Walking Bear

RATTLING IS AN ANCIENT JOURNEY

White Owl painting on the head of my first rattle.

Thunderbird, one of my power spirits, painted on the head of my first rattle

How far back does rattling go? Rattling seems so natural that in my view its origins are lost in the mists of time, back perhaps before Homo sapiens existed, back to our earliest ancestors. Sounds in nature, sounds as calls, sounds as music, sounds in spiritual journeying, and silence and sounds as meditation are perhaps hardwired in us. Rattling is a beautiful process, a play and a door to new perceptions and perspectives.

This book is designed to help you on your journey of listening and rattling. May it be so!

Writing this work has been inspired and guided by Changing Woman, also known as White Shell Woman, an ancient being of wisdom and light.

A clear vision of her came to me many years ago in the mid 1990s in a Shamanic Journey led by my Austrian friend, Unmani. Thank you, Unmani.

In that journey, I went to a sacred place and saw an old woman sitting in front of a fire. I stood by it being purified by its smoke and I saw the woman change from infant to young girl and young woman. She spoke to me and told me to go to the place of the Great Spirit.

Where the place of the Great Spirit was located had already been told to Unmani during her Shamanic training. She had completed a Shamanic training in California and in one of her sweats had picked up a White Shell and had heard the name Manitoba. Someone told her it was a place in Canada: that was all she knew. We eventually discovered our destination in Manitoba. In our inquiry, we came across a beautiful photographic book by Milne on Sacred Places and one of them was called Manitou Abhee, which meant literally, Place of the Great Spirit. It turned out to be part of White Shell Provincial Park in the eastern park of Manitoba!

Manitou Abhee was said to be the place where you could feel the heartbeat of the earth and indeed this is so. It is imbued with the quality of the sacred. There are thousands of stones here set in the form of animals and native people have come here since time unknown for vision quests. Beyond having the status of a provincial park, the site is watched over by native caretakers who ensure the placement of the stones is carefully maintained.

The time in Manitou Abhee was magical. Afterwards, while still in Manitoba, I received the gift of my first rattle. We visited a Native elder, a Grandmother who had a small store with handcrafted items. She was also a rattle maker and after accepting my offering of tobacco agreed to make a rattle designed for my spiritual work.

Author's first rattle,
made by a Grandmother
(Native Elder) in
Manitoba, 1995

It is a beautiful and precious rattle, the container made from moose hide filled with small pebbles and with a deer antler handle. Each side of the moose hide is painted with an image of one of my animal guides, a white owl on one side and the Thunderbird on the other side.

In the last few years, Changing Woman has given guidance in the art of rattling and these practices form part of the background experience for this book.

Thank you, Changing Woman, for the understanding of rattling that has unfolded in the writing of this text.

Wishing each of you who has read this text blessings on your journey, wherever your path leads you!

"You are the space between the stars."

Bo

RESOURCES

I've listed here resources that either support, enrich or expand the work with sound, listening and rattling presented in this book, with the hope they will inspire you and be fruitful avenues of exploration.

Science, Sound and Light

The Sensora | www.sensora.com

This is the high end of sound and light technology. The Sensora is an extraordinary light and sound therapy and meditation chamber, a place to go like a spa for relaxation, healing and meditation. Developed over the past 40 years by physicist, Anadi Martel, and Tantra author and Light Therapist, Ma Premo, this system merges meditation, healing and science. The Sensora is something to be experienced, powerful and deeply relaxing, technology that serves human needs and personal development!

Light Therapies: A Complete Guide to the Healing Power of Light | by Anadi Martel, the physicist who co-created the Sensora system. A must read for anyone who wishes to understand the healing power of light.

La célébration sexuelle | Ma Premo and M. Geet Éthier, Édition de Mortagne. In French. A beautiful book for those who wish to explore using all their senses in intimate relationships.

Healing Sounds - The Power of Harmonics
Jonathan Goldman, Healing Arts Press. A foundational book about sound and its role in healing. Contains an extensive discography describing many sacred and healing recordings.

Active Meditations for Emotional Release and Opening Our Energies

The 4 meditations below designed by Osho are of great help for releasing pent up emotions and stress. They are each a 1-hour process, so they require commitment, but I am including them because they are of such immense value. Some benefits are a greater capacity to witness our thoughts and emotions, freeing ourselves from conditionings, moving our energy, a feeling of well being that resonates throughout the day and opening our hearts.

Dynamic Meditation:

www.osho.com/meditation/osho-active-meditations/
osho-dynamic-meditation

A powerful, early morning meditation for emotional release, clearing and becoming the Watcher.

Kundalini Meditation:

www.osho.com/meditation/osho-active-meditations/
osho-kundalini-meditation

A meditation for freeing one's energy, letting go of stress, loosening up and releasing.

Nataraj meditation:

www.osho.com/meditation/osho-active-meditations/
osho-nataraj-meditation

A dance meditation for moving into the flow.

Devavani Meditation:

www.osho.com/meditation/osho-active-meditations/
osho-devavani-meditation

A gentle meditation for relaxing the mind, brings deep sleep if done before bedtime.

Examples of Brainwave Entrainment Music for Relaxation, Healing and Meditation

Equisync from the Exploration of Consciousness Research Institute (EOC)

https://eocinstitute.org/meditation/

They offer a wide range of Brainwave Entrainment music. Their website provides detailed explanations of the many aspects of the science and art behind their approach.

brain.fm | https://www.brain.fm/

Their home page reads Brain.fm contains patterns that shift your brain state with entrainment. "Our music sounds different—and affects you differently—than any other music."

Jingling Earrings, 1st century CE, Roman, gold and pearl. "Known as crotalia (from the Greek word for rattle or castanets) because the pearl pendants would produce a jingling noise when worn, earrings of this type were extremely popular with Roman ladies."
Source: Metropolitan Museum, New York
Image Public Domain

A Few Terms and Concepts Related to Music and Brainwave Entrainment

Frequency, or pitch, is the number of oscillations or times repeated per second of a sound pressure wave. A bassoon has a much lower frequency than a piccolo, and a baritone singing produces a lower frequency than a soprano.

The great 440 Hz conspiracy, and why all of our music is wrong: Alan Cross

https://globalnews.ca/news/4194106/440-hz-conspiracy-music/

A drole look at various historically competing frequencies: 440 Hz became the standard while the competing 432 Hz, which resonates with 8 Hz (the Schumann Resonance), the documented fundamental electromagnetic "beat" of Earth, was not selected.

Understanding Schumann Resonance

https://neurolaunch.com/schumann-resonance-effect-on-brain/

An overview about Schumann Resonance and its implications for well being and healing.

What is resonance?

https://science.howstuffworks.com/resonance-info.htm

A look at what it means to resonate together.

What Are the Benefits of Listening to Binaural Beats?

Psychology Today, November 20, 2023 Binaural Beats, one of the approaches to create brainwave entrainment, is explained.

How and What We Hear, and How
We Interpret Sound

Musical Illusions and Phantom Words: How Music and Speech Unlock Mysteries of the Brain, Diana Deutsch

The author presents a fascinating overview of what happens in the mind as we listen.

42 Audio Illusions & Phenomena!

A 5-part series on psychoacoustics, Casey Connor, YouTube videos.

John C. Lily - Cogitate, Loop Tape from 1971, Youtube.

Many years ago, I first listened to a loop tape playing the single word "cogitate" repeatedly. It was created by the famous dolphin researcher, John C. Lily, whose work inspired the films *Altered States and Day of the Dolphin.*

Nurse Florence®, How Do We Hear Things?
Michael Stephen Dow.

God's Cricket Chorus
Recorded by Jim Wilson in 1992, YouTube. Here's what crickets sounded like when the sound is stretched out to the equivalent of human singing.

Listen
Gabi Snyder and Stephanie Graegin, Simon & Schuster/Paula Wiseman Books.
A children's book about listening.

Listen to the Universe
https://plus.nasa.gov/video/listen-to-the-universe/

Seated Harp Player, marble, 2800-2700 BCE, Cycladic Culture, Greece. Source: Metropolitan Museum, New York *Image Public Domain*

Music

The Essential Canon of Classical Music
David Dubal, North Point Press. A very helpful reference for those who love classical music.

Music for Healing and Inner Peace
Stephen Halpern | www.stevenhalpernmusic.com
Over many decades Stephen Halpern has created
some of the finest music for relaxation and healing,
incorporating knowledge of brain wave frequencies
and developments in both science and music.

Healing Yourself with Your Own Voice,
Don Campbell, audio cassette, Sounds True.
A classic work of sound healing.

Music of Love and Awareness
Deva Prem and Miten | https://devapremalmiten.com
Wonderful, beautiful mantra music that touches the heart!

Talks with Deuter | https://newearthrecords.com/artists/music-by-deuter/conversations-with-deuter
Deuter is the creator of much-loved meditation music
for Osho Kundalini, Dynamic and other meditations
that has helped support people through these powerful
processes. His music for these meditations, as well as
for Reiki and healing seem organically perfect, as if
transcribed from the divine intelligence.

Music as Vibrational Connective Highways
www.amycamie.com/f/FINAL_PDF-Music_as_Vibrational_Connective_Highways,_Camie,_Nov-Dec,_2017_(1).pdf
An article exploring how music transmits the
vibration of the musician - their thoughts and feelings
- to the listener.

Trees and Listening

The Attentive Heart: Conversations with Trees
Stephanie Kaza, Shambhala
A lovely, thoughtful exploration.

Secrets from the Lives of Trees
Goelitz, Jeffrey, Boulder Creek, California,
Planetary Publications, 1991 (out of print)
A sensitive book about connecting and listening to trees.

Plant Wave | https://plantwave.com
Plant Wave is a device to listen to plants, which
works by converting changes in electrical
conductivity of plants into audio, allowing trees,
flowers, plants, and mushrooms to sing.

Voices from the Past

The Oldest Voices We Can Still Hear
Kings and Things, YouTube video.

Historical Voices of Famous People
Cyprian Sieńkowski, YouTube video.

<< Butternut
(Juglans cinerea)

Meditation

The Book of Secrets: 112 Meditations to Discover the Mystery Within, Osho, St. Martin's Griffin.
Osho's elucidation of the 112 seed techniques of tantra meditation are of incalculable value. He shares invaluable insights and practical indications, making this a profound How-to Book, a roadmap that enables the reader to experiment with these techniques with a fuller understanding of their psychology, spiritual import and the markers and milestones that help us stay on the path.

Meditations , J. Krishnamurti, Shambhala.
This is a collection of brief excerpts from Krishnamurti's books and talks on meditation.

A Guide to Awareness and Tranquillity
William Samuel, Butterfly Publishing House.
I love this book and the author's insights. He shares
a special story related to the theme of this book, an
experience of sound and transformation as a soldier
during the Korean War.

The Everyday Meditator
Osho, Tuttle Pub.
A brilliant book, offering many practical meditations
for different times of the day. Humming as a
meditation is described.

**Poetry: The Great Undoing - Dissolving the me
into the infinite**
Stuart Schwartz, Non-Duality Press.

Man Praying, Our Lady of Guadalupe Shrine, Johnstown, Cape Breton, Nova Scotia, Canada

Prayer

Jesus on Prayer
Art Nuernberg, The E.I. School of Biblical Training.
The author reflects on the nature of prayer as taught by Jesus.

The Frame of Mind in the Lord's Prayer
https://imagicworldview.blogspot.com/2017/01/the-frame-of-mind-in-lords-prayer-and.html
Discusses various understandings of the Lord's Prayer given by Jesus. Contains Ferrar Fenton's translation from Greek of The Lord's Prayer (from The Complete Bible in Modern English) as well as an Aramaic translation.

Neville Goddard - The Complete Collection: The reference book by Neville Goddard with all 15 books, radio lectures and lessons
An awakened consciousness, Neville Goddard brings many insights to such areas as prayer, imagination, and manifestation.

Jewish Meditation: A Practical Guide
Aryeh Kaplan, Schocken.
Amongst the many meditations described by Kaplan is that of prayer. Many prayers were designed as meditation processes to connect to the deepest Source.

The Prayer of the Kabbalist:
The 42-Letter Name of God
Yehuda Berg, Kabbalah Publishing.
The author takes us line by line through the powerful Ana Bekoach prayer, revealing its meaning and purpose.

Kabbalah of Prayer
Shulamit Elson, Lindisfarne Books.
Of note is the author's development of meditative
"Sound Prayers."

The Power of Prayer (Channeling Brain Waves Through Dhikr)
Ahmed Hulusi
The author is a Turkish, Islamic thinker who shares
his experience and insight into prayer.

Nine Prayers given by the Buddhist Master Thich Nhat Hanh
Simple, gentle, meaningful prayers given by Thich
Nhat Hanh.

100 Questions about Ho'oponopono
Mabel Katz, Your Business Press
The prayer known as the "Ho'oponopono"
(HO-oh-Po-no-Po-no) helps us in an often difficult
area, forgiveness.

Self-Inquiry

Who Am I? Sri Ramana Maharshi
The great Indian mystic, Ramana Maharshi, responds to questions about the direct method of knowing oneself.

AHAM - Sharing the Teaching of Self-Inquiry
www.aham.com

American Mystic – Memoirs of a Happy Man
A. Ramana, Inquiry Books.
Based on interviews with A. Ramana by Saroja Poilblan, about his life and awakening. A. Ramana was an American spiritual teacher in the tradition of Self-Inquiry given by the Indian mystic Ramana Maharshi.

The Mystery

Synchronicity: An Acausal Connecting Principle
Carl Gustav Jung
Synchronicity is said to be God's way of showing us that the divine intelligence responds and plays a role in our lives. We are much more likely to observe the synchronistic unfolding of events when we meditate, pray, listen and fall in tune with existence.

Sacred Places in North America: A Journey into the Medicine Wheel
Courtney Milne, Harry N. Abrams.
Sacred places in North America beautifully photographed.

Cow Rattle, pottery,
1550 – 1295 BCE,
Egypt.
Source: Metropolitan
Museum, New York
Image Public Domain

Rattles and Early Musical Instruments

How to Make Drums, Tomtoms & Rattles – Primitive Percussion Instruments for Modern Use
Bernard S. Mason, Dover Publications, New York.

The rattle: A treasured baby toy
www.musee-mccord-stewart.ca/en/blog/rattle-treasured-toy/

STONE AGE: 3.3 MILLION TO 5,000 YEARS AGO

The earliest musical instruments to be discovered thus far are flutes, dating back as far as 60,000 years ago.

Paleolithic flutes: the oldest musical instruments
https://en.wikipedia.org/wiki/Paleolithic_flute

Divje Babe flute: the Possibility That Neanderthals Played Music | https://en.wikipedia.org/wiki/Divje_Babe_flute
Although the evidence is controversial, the idea that the Neanderthals had a musical culture 50,000 to 60,000 years ago is intriguing.

Hear the world's oldest instrument, the 50,000 year old neanderthal flute
https://www.classicfm.com/discover-music/instruments/flute/worlds-oldest-instrument-neanderthal-flute/

19 Of the Oldest Musical Instruments in the World
https://hellomusictheory.com/learn/oldest-instruments/

What Did the Stone Age Sound Like?
www.discovermagazine.com/planet-earth/what-did-the-stone-age-sound-like

8,000 Years Ago, Stone Age People Donned Elk-Tooth Ornaments During Spirited Dance Sessions
www.smithsonianmag.com/smart-news/elk-tooth-ornaments-reveal-ancient-dance-moves-180977902/

BRONZE AGE: 5,000 TO 1,400 YEARS AGO (1,200 BC)

Echoes of Ancient Children: 4,200-Year-Old Rattle Discovered in Turkey
www.ancient-origins.net/news-history-archaeology/echoes-ancient-children-4200-year-old-rattle-discovered-turkey-006557

4,000-year-old Children's Rattle Crafted as Bear Cub's Head: And it Still Rattles!
www.ancient-origins.net/news-history-archaeology/4000-year-old-childrens-rattle-crafted-bear-cubs-head-and-it-still-rattles-021036

"We are born of love; Love is our mother."

Rumi

CONTRIBUTORS TO THIS BOOK

Unmani Lenger

Books by authors mentioned by Unmani:

Fire in the Head: Shamanism and the Celtic Spirit, Tom Cowan

Shamanic Journeying, Sandra Ingerman, Sounds True Adult.

Soul Retrieval: Mending the Fragmented, Sandra Ingerman, HarperOne.

Water Blessing Song: Nee bee wah bow - Algonquin Water Song Sung by Women
www.singthewatersong.com/songlyrics

Sean Walking Bear – Master Rattle Maker

Rattles from Sean Walking Bear may be found at the following two websites:

Sunreed Instruments
| sunreed.com |

The Rattle Maker
| www.therattlemaker.com |

Tomson Highway

Tomson Highway - Composer, Playwright, Author, Pianist
https://tomsonhighway.com/

About Tomson Highway
www.thecanadianencyclopedia.ca/en/article/highway-tomson

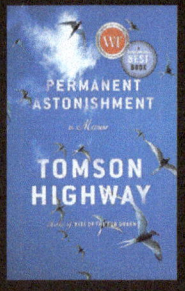

Permanent Astonishment: Growing Up Cree in the Land of Snow and Sky
Tomson Highway, Anchor Canada.
A beautiful life story filled with inspiration and wonder.

Laughing with the Trickster: On Sex, Death, and Accordions (The CBC Massey Lectures), 2022

Author Daniel Tigner

Daniel is author of 8 books, including the present book on the art of deep listening. He is co-creator of Canadian Forest Tree Essences, described on the following pages.

The Art of Grant Tigner, 1990
Daniel's father, Grant Tigner (1921-1999), was a fine landscape and portrait painter.

Sam and the Sea Monsters,
Julie Sutton and Daniel Tigner.
A fictional, sports story for young teens.

The Time of Your Life, Everyone Has a Story,
Gayle Jabour and Daniel Tigner
Interviews with 50 to 90+ year olds about their current life.

American Mystic – Memoirs of a Happy Man,
A. Ramana, Inquiry Books.

Trees, Healing, and You: Guided Imagery, Poems, Stories, & Other Empowering Tools
A compendium of writings about trees and consciousness by Kimberly Burnham, Celine Cloutier, Daniel Tigner, Bassia Alexander, Margo Royce and Jim Conroy.

Tae Kwon Do, Daniel Tigner with his wife Maryse and daughter Sepporah, 2019.

Photo: Saroja Poilblan >>

VIBRATIONAL TREE ESSENCES

Canadian Forest Tree Essences

In the lineage of Bach Flower Remedies, the vibrational tree essences created by Canadian Forest Tree Essences are plant infusions in water that hold the vibrational recording or resonance of trees. Resonance affects us in many ways, but primarily at an emotional and soul level.

"What are Tree Essences?
Vibrational Tree Essences are meticulously crafted liquid extracts, typically administered orally, with the primary objective of fostering emotional and spiritual well-being. Their efficacy lies in their ability to nourish the energy field of an individual or animal through their positive resonance, thereby facilitating the maintenance of inner equilibrium."

Canadian Forest Tree Essences | www.essences.ca

**Canadian Forest Tree Essences – Healing Through the Natural Resonance of Trees (1998)
The Tree Essences Guidebook (2016)**

"How do I listen to others?
As if everyone were my master speaking
to me his cherished last words."

— Hafiz, 14th century Sufi poet

Daniel Tigner, Inquiry Books
www.inquirybooks.com
If you have any questions, thoughts, or feedback,
I'd love to hear from you!

Email: **info@inquirybooks.com**

This book is set in Hightower, a typeface designed
by Tobias Frere-Jones.